Life in Our Black Skin

Why Racism Prevails in America

DARRYL SMITH JR.

Contents

Introduction

RACISM HAS DEEP roots. And I should know.

I am a black man living in America. I am an Iraq War veteran and served in the army for ten years. Serving this nation has given me a diverse outlook on life and my country. I can see how life is to be cherished and appreciated.

I have partaken in several run-ins with law enforcement when I was a youth. Driving from work, I received numerous tickets for various things. I was pulled over for driving through a white neighborhood because I didn't have a fancy car.

This type of systemic oppression from the government is crippling our society—the continuous struggle we suffer through as a black man or woman in America. I feel, as do many others, like I have to be on my best behavior and avoid police when probable.

There are many things wrong with our nation, and many things that are great in our nation. I want to talk about the real issues that are affecting the racial rift within America. I would like for America to be a true united nation. As a united nation, we can ease the tension of racial issues that are prevalent in our society.

I want to enlighten the people of America—black, white, Asian, Latino, Hispanic, Native American—about why there is so much of an ethnic divide in America. *Life in Our Black Skin* is based on my life and how I see America. I have used several facts throughout this book to justify my anger toward blacks as well as white Americans.

I want Americans to stop being naïve about what is going on in their country. I would like for white people to take responsibility for what has happened for hundreds of years. I want to see white people just as upset as blacks are so that we know they see that there is a problem within our borders.

I think that the majority of Americans see blacks as all the same, and I want for Americans not to judge blacks by the skin they see or by the clothes they wear. Each black person isn't the same, just as each white person isn't the same. White people, to my knowledge, don't judge each other by their skin so why are minorities any different?

I can understand how other non-black Americans can see blacks as thugs with dreadlocks and flashing their guns as ignorant because of the behavior that is displayed and publicized through the media and television. TV reality shows paint the most ignorant picture of black people who do not understand that they are the face white America potentially sees. The daily news displays blacks committing the worst of crimes. The news also words black criminals differently than white criminals.

I'm aware that many white people aren't racist. Those who are not racist need to stop hiding their voices and stand up to those who are oppressing their fellow Americans. White America must realize that black America has PTSD (post-traumatic stress disorder). Black America has been beaten and battered. We have been used like an old shirt that is now a rag.

White Americans state, "I'm not racist. I didn't have slaves." I have heard these idioms a lot from white people as well as many other ethnicities. If you are a person who thinks like this, you might want to be real with yourself and realize that you feel the guilt. The feeling of guilt means you do understand the actions of your ancestors, whether you like it or not. Now you may not have had slaves and you may not feel that you are bigoted, which is understandable. On the other hand, white America can't look blacks in the face and say these things knowing that some of your families *did* have slaves. If you have family members who are saying, "Niggas are stupid and steal, and they are thugs because of the music they listen to and the clothes they wear"—if this type of rhetoric is being said in your presence and if you have not stood up to the extremists and state that "all black Americans are not like that," then you're just as guilty as the bigoted.

This book is intended to get the public to talk about the real issues that are plaguing America, issues that we as a society are evading. I essentially would like for all ethnic groups to be proactive in their fellow Americans' fight for equivalent justice.

My message is that blacks in America need to wake up and stop expecting for someone to help you; it's not going to happen. The thought process that someone is going to help you is not a feasible way of thinking. This book may make you feel uncomfortable or upset you. I might talk about blacks and whites a lot in this book, but it's for all ethnicities to read and to get a clear and truthful understanding of the society we all live in. Take my words for a grain of salt or pounds of gold.

Americans have to coexist in this nation. If we cannot coexist with one another, racial conflicts will never end.

Chapter 1: The Downfall of Blacks in America

FROM 1984 TO today, many things have changed. From pay phones on the sidewalks to cell phones that fit in your pocket. From computers that took up your entire kitchen table to tablets that can fit in a folder. Oversized boom boxes to ridiculously small iPods.

But one thing that hasn't changed since the 1980s is the life of a black man in America. Life as a black man has only gotten harder. In the '80s, a big crack and heroin epidemic began—the beginning of the collapse of the black race as a whole, in my opinion. A collapse, because the choices being made crippled the black community. Since the 1980s, it is a fact that blacks, primarily black men, have been arrested more than any other ethnicity for drug possession. It is also a known fact that whites use drugs more often, but are detained significantly less.[1]

Whites in the 1980s were using drugs more than blacks, so why is it that these white suburban folks were not being arrested more? If police knew that white America was using drugs more often, shouldn't they be arrested more? Where is the logic in this? There isn't. I would reason that a smart police chief would be setting up police stings to catch those who are using these hard drugs regularly.

But that wasn't the case.

The punitive criminalization of drugs by the United States government was not only tearing down black neighborhoods but also the black family dynamic. This criminalization affected the black community by having harsher drug sentencing and the destruction of the community.

Many black family members have overdosed from the use of drugs. The sharing of needles in the communities from using heroin also spiked AIDS in the black community.[2]

The fact that black men are being arrested and rounded up like cattle is frightening. The alarming rate of these arrests affects everything from neighborhoods

---

[1] http://www.pewresearch.org/fact-tank/2014/07/18/chart-of-the-week-the-black-white-gap-in-incarceration-rates/

[2] http://www.pbs.org/wgbh/frontline/article/timeline-30-years-of-aids-in-black-america/

to families. There are little boys and girls who may never see their parents again because of an overdose from narcotics or because their father is being detained for his activities in dealing drugs. I state this because the rate of black men arrested for selling drugs in the 80s to present has quadrupled.[3] The frequent arrests of black men bring another matter that leads to fatherless children.

At the rate blacks are being locked up and slain, there is a possibility society could have had the next Steve Jobs or Albert Einstein. Think of all the imaginable things that could have been invented if the next genius had not been shot and killed at a traffic stop for a taillight. Blacks are more worried about getting money while hustling and killing each other in the process. Yet blacks get upset when a white cop kills a black man. Those who do have the power to stop the unnecessary harassment of black men have not altered laws that can fix the problem.

Black men were and are at a major disadvantage from the time they are born in America. They are born black and many times, born with one or *no* parents. If you have one parent, it's more than likely that your father may be in prison or dead. There are some fathers who just don't claim their children, sadly. These black children grow up fast and some have to

---

[3] https://www.hrw.org/sites/default/files/reports/us0508_1.pdf

3

provide for themselves and their siblings. Many of those who have to support themselves may have to work sooner, which doesn't allow for those young men to go to college. The repercussions from black children not being able to go to college entails that the lifestyle they wanted for themselves or their family wouldn't be as they may have planned in their future. Consequently, young black men may also become a part of the unjust judicial system. The black male has to be conscious that school is the only savior to get you out of your current horrid conditions. College will give you knowledge to help you succeed in life and get out of poverty.

In the 1980s, there were at least factory jobs. You could throw a rock and find a factory, whereas now, there are hardly any factory jobs. Nowadays, there is *no* such thing as factory occupations. There aren't many jobs that pay well without a minimum of a bachelor's degree.[4] Those who own corporations sent many factory positions to China or some other country to avoid labor cost. The closing of factory jobs made for more unemployed blacks in society.

Is there a reason that there are only five to ten

----

[4]   https://www.creditwritedowns.com/2012/05/chart-of-the-day-us-manufacturing-unemployment-1960-2012.html

black CEOs in the Fortune 500?[5] How is this possible in 2016? There are not enough blacks within their field to get the recognition that is warranted. I'm sure there are qualified blacks who can accomplish the same or better, as their counterpart—whites. Is this not disturbing to white America, the massive difference of the lack of blacks in their prospective career fields?

Whites get a pass on certain things because they are white. We know this as *white privilege*. White privileged people can yell and tell off cops without having to worry about getting shot. The difference is the pigment of the skin that the police observe. Whites are oblivious to the world around them. Black issues do not directly affect them; therefore, they don't care. If whites cared, they would intervene more often and help their fellow Americans.

So how can white Americans get involved? Help by getting congress and the senate to modify laws that will stop profiling. Tell police to stop with the quotas every month—the quotas that are forcing police to profile. Whites can also stop being so afraid of blacks. Black culture is different than white culture, but there isn't a reason that whites cannot communicate with blacks without starting an immense commotion.

Blacks shouldn't have to concern themselves

---

[5]   http://money.cnn.com/2015/01/29/news/economy/mcdonalds-ceo-diversity/

about the clothes they wear. Blacks shouldn't have to worry about wearing a hoodie or their jeans sagging when they leave their house because of how they may be perceived by whites and police. Blacks have to make sure they wear the proper clothing when walking around their own neighborhood because of gang violence. People in these gang zones have to avoid wearing certain colors. This is baffling to me. So if you are a black person, you have to beware of what you're wearing no matter what the reason or where you are going? Blacks cannot wear a hoodie when it's cold outside because it will give the appearance of someone who is mischievous.

There aren't many things to do in the ghettos and projects of America except for guns, drugs, and life-threatening violence. When I was fourteen years old, I had a summer job. We had playgrounds with basketball courts. The basketball courts had no nets on the rim, but that was okay. The economics of this country also has a lot to do with the current state of many poor communities: Latino, white, and black alike. If there were more occupations, even just summer jobs for the youth in America in major cities, there would be less violence and poverty.

The government needs to invest in the innovation of community centers where kids can go play sports and do crafts for a few hours. Communities can also have more programs to employ students for the summer to help them get job experience for their future. These children are now the product of their environment, and you can only expect so much with an indistinct possibility of a future. If the government invests more into the future of America, there will be better possibilities for all Americans.

Chapter 2: Cops Abusing Power

THE TRUTH IS: some police abuse their power. Cops in America racial profile even if they do not like to admit it. Police have a hazardous job, and I understand that, but an officer of the law has to be able to use some restraint when they draw their firearm.

I was twenty years old when I deployed to Iraq, and we had to use restraint from shooting the terrorists. We had to have positive sights on a weapon or actions that may have seemed threatening before acting. Soldiers could not go into countries and just shoot anything that moved—there are rules of engagement. I am sure the police have these rules, but many of them choose not to use this technique.

Being black in America, we have to become smarter by reading more. Learn the laws better than those who are in power to prosper. If we do not, then we will stay under individuals who don't care about blacks or "niggers," as some say when we aren't looking or when they are behind closed doors. The minority of white Americans that are racist speaks for the majority when the majority does not stand up for their fellow citizens. But if we know the laws, this will make it easier to defend ourselves. Knowing the laws will help with court trials or interactions with the police. This will make it better to defend ourselves with the knowledge that has been acquired.

I would like for my son to go driving with his friends and not have a white man shoot him because he listens to his music too loud. Like forty-seven-year-old Michael Dunn, who was convicted of first-degree murder for shooting seventeen-year-old Jordan Davis over the loud rap music coming out of his SUV in November 2012.[6] Being black in America is a crime in and of itself.

Another miserable example is Tamir Rice, a twelve-year-old boy who was shot in Cleveland, Ohio, in 2014.[7] I can't believe a child was shot without the police saying, "Hey, what are you doing? Stop! Drop the weapon!" The cops instead pull up on the sidewalk and shoot a child who was black only *because* he was black. The child had a toy gun. If that isn't racism, I don't know what is.

In the 1980s, 90s, and at this time, you have to

---

[6]   http://www.nydailynews.com/news/crime/florida-man-life-prison-killing-teen-loud-music-article-1.1978021

[7]   http://abcnews.go.com/US/cleveland-cops-recklessly-shot-boy-12-toy-gun/story?id=27402837

realize cops were treating black men the same. The only difference now is that social media and cell phones can record clearly and quickly.

Let's take a look at Rodney King in California in 1991.[8] He had led the police on a car chase and as he gave himself up, he was brutally attacked and beaten by LAPD's finest. If one person had not been recording the incident, those Los Angeles police would have gotten away with the ass-whooping that hospitalized this man. I'm not saying he was a saint, but there's a line—and they crossed it.

The amount of unarmed, defenseless blacks who have been slain by police is scandalous. The next shocking thing is that most of these police get indicted for their police misconduct. I'll call it what it is: unjustified murders. Once indicted, most of these police receive no prison sentence and remain officers of the law. There have been countless shootings and not enough police who have gone to prison for their irresponsible actions. I honestly do not understand how this can occur in an allegedly *fair* judicial system.

Thankfully, there are some communities that are trying to make progress. New York recently got rid of "stop and frisk," which was only hurting the already tarnished image of blacks. It also caused blacks to be more hostile toward cops. Cops by human nature

---

[8] https://en.wikipedia.org/wiki/Rodney_King

profile people. Cops see a black person and think the worst of a race because of a small few who chose to do wrong. Meanwhile, many other blacks work hard and try to make a better life for themselves.

I myself was planning on becoming a police officer. I was in the military for ten years so I thought this would be a respectable career. Until I saw that cops were killing innocent, unarmed black men while their actions were covered up by other cops. I didn't want to be a part of the slaughtering of unarmed black men. I understand that the police took an oath that they would protect each other, as well as the law, but if you're upholding the law, you should know that your comrades' actions are wrong. Police need to be held accountable for their actions. What the police departments are doing by covering the wrongdoings for those who have committed a crime is appalling. It makes the police who are covering up the corruption just as guilty as the officer who has committed the crime.

Why haven't cops been trained to use the kill shot as a last resort? They have Tasers, but they chose not to use them when dealing with blacks or they purposely overuse the Tasers, causing severe damage to the victim. When I was in the army and in Iraq, if you took a shot, the first shot was a warning. Then the next shot was to disable the person or vehicle, and then the kill shot. The army used an escalation of force. I do not see the police trying to use this escalation of force. If they would use escalation of force tactics and be trained more efficiently, this would eliminate the deaths of more unarmed black men and Americans in general.

It looks as if cops are killings blacks for them simply being black and at the wrong place at the wrong time. We are supposed to be calm, though, because he "shouldn't have done this or that." Cops, you've got to do better. Shooting an unarmed black man in the back? There is not an excuse for those actions.

I would advise black men who get pulled over or confronted by the police to record the interaction and comply with them no matter if they are in the wrong or right. It sounds like being a sellout or being weak, but I'd rather live to see my next birthday and my kids' next Christmas. I want my children to still have a father. If I were to take the other route, bucking up to the police and getting shot over a traffic violation, then that would be a senseless way to die. I shouldn't have to walk on eggshells to survive a simple traffic stop from the police.

Most cops think blacks are always up to no good. The culture of cops in the majority of major cities is to profile minorities.[9] Police deal with criminals all day

---

[9] https://www.washingtonpost.com/news/wonk/wp/2016/07/08/the-big-question-about-why-police-pull-over-so-many-black-drivers/

because that is their job. Police *do* profile people just by looking at someone. I believe that the police should change their tactics and get to know the community in which they work. A suggestion that will help the police would be to live in the neighborhood or closer to the neighborhood in which the officer patrols. If police officers did live closer to the area, it would make for better relations with the community. The police would have a better insight on how to approach certain situations. When cops have public community functions, make sure people know you're having one and that the community is invited. Don't have community functions and only police officers' families and friends in attendance.

Solving tension between blacks and police officers begins with strengthening our community and forming a good relationship.

Chapter 3: The Government's Agenda

I BELIEVE THE government is the main cause for the boom in the 1980's drug epidemic. The United States' war on drugs is another war this nation has started that they choose not to end. Monetarily, it doesn't make sense for the US to do so.

Manuel Noriega is a known drug dealer from Panama. Noriega worked with the United States until they could no longer control his actions. As this occurred, there are a lot of people in the US who know about this situation. Why would the government work with a known drug dealer?

The US has many resources at its fingertips but chooses not to confront the drugs that are coming into the US through its borders. It doesn't benefit the government monetarily to do anything about the current flow of drugs. If you stop the flow of drugs into the US, there wouldn't be as many people in prison. The lesser number of people in prison would affect the government's paycheck—the money that comes from taxpayers who go to work every day. The

US would have to find another way to swindle and shake down the American populous.

America has been fighting the war on drugs for a long time, and it's still an ongoing fight. The US hiring a known drug lord to help them stop drugs from coming to America seems unrealistic. I wouldn't hire someone knowing they are going to somehow benefit from working with myself or have a negative effect on my nation's well-being.

The War on Drugs began in 1971 with President Richard Nixon. A few years later, the US goes to war with Panama over drugs *and* the informant Noriega, whom they thought they were helping. But Noriega was using America for his own success.[10] The information the government was getting from Noriega wasn't worth the lives of thousands that both the US and Panama lost. It wasn't worth the millions in prison and thousands of deaths caused by the drug trade that is influenced by the American government.

The consequences of the United States allowing drugs to come in to the States has crippled the inner cities. As we know, many inner cities have a large black population. Every major city in America is ravaged with illegal drugs. The government acts as if

---

[10]

https://web.stanford.edu/class/e297c/poverty_prejudice/paradox/htele.html

they had nothing to do with the current state of drugs in black communities.

Marijuana is a relatively mild, non-addictive drug with limited hallucinogenic properties. Legalizing or decriminalizing marijuana will reduce the number of people who get arrested for selling it illegally. This would reduce the number of arrests, meaning we'll also have fewer people in prison for non-violent crimes.

The United States made a huge blunder in trusting crime boss Manuel Noriega. The War on Drugs is a joke that isn't funny and is costing thousands of lives to be affected daily. If America really wanted to stop the drugs being trafficked into the US, they would do so intelligently and efficiently. I think that the government can add more personnel to the border patrol and coast guard to stop the flow of drugs coming into our country on all the borders.

Chapter 4: The Cycle

THE CYCLE IS a series of systematic oppression in America that only minorities can see and are effected by. Those who are in power want blacks to stay in prison to keep us divided. If this isn't the truth, then they need to show the black community that our government leaders actually care. Blacks need to start seeing what is directly in front of them, or they will blindly keep losing freedom.

The cycle begins at birth for black Americans. As a black child, the situation you are brought up in is not in your favor to succeed. A black child goes to a school that is below the standards of the state. I'm sure that many predominantly white schools do not come close to the disorder of black public schools. Meanwhile, white kids go to better public schools and the rich kids go to private schools.

Brown v. Board of Education is a case that allowed for blacks to go to the same school as whites in 1954. Whites schools, on average, receive across the country $334 more for every white student compared to non-white students.[11]

Jonathan Kozol described the difference between schools that are miles apart. Kozol described two schools: one that was predominately black and another school that was predominately white.[12] The black school had a biology class without a laboratory or the equipment to dissect frogs. The same school had a word processor class without computers. The nearby suburban school had functional biology classes and computers that had software that allowed the students to study stocks.

I was fortunate enough to go to a white elementary school. I could tell a difference from being around my family that did not go to the same school. They went to black schools in Philadelphia. When I went to high school, it changed to a predominately black school, but the school was still better than the schools that my family went to in the city. I was ahead in certain subjects that had not been taught to them for whatever reason. I know now that schools are the reason blacks are not a huge factor in the job force or colleges other than sports. If the government invested

---

[11]

https://www.americanprogress.org/issues/education/news/2012/08/22/32862/students-of-color-still-receiving-unequal-education/

[12] http://www.brookings.edu/research/articles/1998/03/spring-education-darling-hammond

more in the future of black Americans other than building more prisons to contain them, blacks would have a fighting chance.

When a black child becomes a teen in major cities, they are likely to be surrounded by drugs, guns, and things that can land a black person in a penitentiary. The black community needs to work together to get these black teenagers something to do, rather than hanging out with the local drug dealers on the corners. The adults who are around need to become more responsible for their child's actions as well as others who may not have any support system at home. The prevention measures have to be a community affair.

We've wasted a lot of energy on gun control. I said *wasted* because gun control does not stop the buying of illegal guns in the hoods of inner cities. Gun control isn't going to stop black-on-black violence. White America needs to be serious about wanting to change and progress. Criminals of any ethnicity don't care about the laws.

Now this is where the cycle becomes more concentrated. A black teen released from jail cannot find a job or has to support his or her family, which then leads them to doing criminal activities. These criminal activities will lead many black youths back to prison. It's like the movie *Groundhog Day*. Once you're in the system of incarceration, it's hard to get out. The cycle keeps repeating itself—and it's becoming vicious and risky.

It's an immense cycle that's taking place in black America. Blacks sell the drugs that are being imported illegally because of numerous reasons. Then blacks get arrested for the selling of drugs—in which this cycle becomes a part of the judicial system. The government is getting paid from the incarceration of people in general. Blacks are the ones who have a commanding presence in jails. The government makes millions of dollars, which is due to the cycle of black folks who are constantly going through in America. So the cycle that I mentioned keeps repeating itself again and again.

Young black folks need to realize that following those who are doing wrong means you'll end up in the wrong place—like prison or a coffin. It's never too late to change your destiny. It's not too late to be anything you chose to put your mind to. There is a black president, so there is a chance—you just have to want it more and follow through with your plan. Right now, I think some blacks feel entitled to things that aren't theirs. No one is going to just give it to you. You have to remember this is America, so nothing is free.

There is a cycle of the enslavement mentality within the black community. If you are someone who still works for someone else and you have no desire to own your own business, that is a slave mentality. Blacks need to have their own companies, banks, real estate, and other businesses that will make them successful.

It's time to work together and stop despising each other. Hating each other is obviously not working.

Chapter 5: A Black Life Scenario

JUSTICE IS SUPPOSED to be blind, but somehow, it can tell that your skin has color: the wrong color. In this chapter, I will give you a detailed scenario on how black people get caught in the judicial system. I'll explain the effects of black families that have been through similar situations. The same system that states, "You're innocent until proven guilty." This same system, when talking about blacks, is guilty until they are proven innocent. Judges are known to give blacks a harsher sentencing for no reason.

The fathers who are in jail can't get out of jail because they cannot afford real lawyers or because their bond is set unreasonably high. The appointed court lawyers don't get paid as much as law firm lawyers, so they tend not to care as much about the cases they are appointed. These lawyers always make plea deals instead of fighting for your innocence.

These black men have been convicted of felony crimes like selling marijuana or possession of controlled substances. For this reason, they cannot become a part of society. Society has a stigmatism about convicted criminals. Things we take for granted are stripped once you are a convicted felon. You can't vote as a convicted felon or get a good job.

On job applications, they ask, "Have you been convicted of a crime?" In most cases, you have to disclose the alleged criminal act. Some employers who see this automatically put the application in the trash or have a software system they use to sort through applications and if *felony* is checked, it repeatedly discards the application.

Convicted felons who are out on parole or just getting out of jail have to get a job. There are several programs that allow for felons to get jobs. Many of these jobs are not good-paying ones, though. The inability to get decent jobs because of a non-violent crime at the age of eighteen follows you for several years. This makes it harder for blacks, as well as any ethnicity, to get jobs and keep them out of prison. Many blacks don't even know that you can get some convictions expunged from your record with time. Some felons get out of prison and do not have a high school diploma or a GED, which shrinks their career potentials.

This leaves the mother of the children in which their significant other has been sentenced to serve several years behind bars. The mother has to care for the children by herself. There are many good black mothers who handle their business when it comes to taking care of their children. They might have to work two jobs to get by. Let's not forget that some mothers also do not have a college degree because they had children way too early.

The problem is that the child is born into a situation because two people, who know right from wrong, keep choosing to do wrong. Here is the issue: the child is here and Dad is absent due to him being in prison, so Mom has to work with whatever job she can get.

Moms is at work, and the oldest child (a boy) needs money to help pay bills or to eat, so he steps outside of his house. He sees the society surrounding him. He sees boys getting money for selling drugs. The money that these street entrepreneurs make is better than working a minimum-wage job. So why not try hustling? They make more money hustling than working at Walmart. America, ask yourself, why would I work at a place where I'm going to work crazy hours and still be broke? At this point, the boy will take his chances being in the streets selling controlled substances.

If you are the oldest female and your mom is always working, you're probably going to get caught up with the wrong people because you have little to no supervision. The lack of direction allows for the teen to make wrong decisions. There are young females who are attracted to these drug dealers. Young females see them as popular, and they see their money. Then she will become pregnant and nine months later, there is another black child born. Black teen females are 34.9 births per one thousand teenage females, so every 35 out of one thousand black teenage women become pregnant before 18 years of age.[13] God made somebody to make condoms, but people still don't use them and end up having five kids with a man who has been convicted of a felony three times.

This black man can't ever get a real job and ends up back in jail because of unpaid child support or for committing another crime. You aren't cool anymore. You're a thirty-plus-year-old black man, your kids are fatherless, but you got the new Lebrons and Jordans—how does that make sense to anyone? You could have saved some of that money for your child's education, but you didn't. You chose to use your money frivolously on some useless material clothing.

---

[13] http://www.hhs.gov/ash/oah/adolescent-health-topics/reproductive-health/teen-pregnancy/trends.html

Chapter 6: The Lack of Schooling

PUBLIC SCHOOLS IN black communities are nothing like schools in other communities in America. Public school teachers get paid around $40,000 on average and they have classes with more than twenty-five students per class.[14] There was a study conducted by the *New York Times* that showed inner city teachers being paid less than schools in the suburbs.[15] How can children learn in a congested classroom with one teacher? The answer is: you cannot learn in that manner. Each student will not receive the amount of attention that is needed to pass the class because of overcrowding.

Schools have issues that come from the federal

14

https://www.psea.org/uploadedFiles/LegislationAndPolitics/Vision/Visio
n_ReduceClassSizes.pdf

15 http://www.nytimes.com/2000/05/31/nyregion/on-teacher-pay-city-vs-
suburbs-isn-t-that-simple.html

government. The funding for schools has been cut significantly in the past few years. Schools are also more worried about state testing than actual learning. But schools are not solely to blame for delinquency in the black community. The educators in charge of funding should be able to find other ways to fund their schools for children in poverty.

The reasoning behind delinquency in the black community are poor schools and parenting. In society, everyone is quick to blame others for their lack of supervision of their children. I think parents in the black community need to be accountable and start taking control of their child's future. Delinquency stems from the environment of a child. I don't think children need to be in fear of their parents. I think black children who are raised to respect their parent(s) and others will also have respect for authority. The government also needs to begin fixing the problem of delinquency by taking money from building new prisons and putting it into school systems and investing in the future of America.

There are teens who don't want to be in school because they aren't learning anything. There are teens with family members who haven't graduated high school. In some public schools, there are teachers who fear for their lives. These schools are made up of black children who don't listen to anyone of authority. Black kids get mad because the teacher said, "You're wrong, so sit down." So the kid decides to hit the teacher or talk back, yelling obscenities. I know why this happens because their parents haven't taught them to respect their elders or they realize that they are not going to make it to an age where school matters.

Black children are institutionalized when they start school. Schools have metal detectors and bars on the windows. I know white schools don't have metal detectors or bars on the windows.[16] The bars aren't to keep the children in; it's to keep the crack heads out. Crack heads break into the schools and steal the only learning tools that the school has for these poverty-stricken children so that they can get high.

The separation of students who grow up in a poor society has many disadvantages for these types of students. When they grow up in depraved neighborhoods, they're labeled before the first day of school. I can understand how teachers could easily label students, but it doesn't make it right! The students are labeled by the way they talk and dress, and by their racial background. These students are not given a true chance in life. The teachers don't care, and why would the student care if he or she passes class or even goes to school at all?

This is when you have students who become truant and delinquents. I also say that parents should try to give their child the best education they can. I

---

[16] http://www.edweek.org/ew/articles/2011/08/31/02security.h31.html

know it's hard because some parents can barely pay the rent, let alone send their child to a private school. But this is my point: blacks must change their attitude toward life, stop the subliminal mental enslavement of ourselves, make our own jobs, make our own money, and get our own education.

It has been said that students who wear uniforms usually receive better grades than those who wear dress-down clothes.[17] If you're not wearing the latest style, then you're not considered to be a cool kid. Students nowadays are more concerned with how they look for Snapchat and Instagram. Students are more worried about the latest apparel than their grades. Social media outlets, such as YouTube, are where they can watch their favorite music artist videos, which tells children what the newest fads are. If you're a student and you don't have these clothes that these superstars wear, you could potentially be made a mockery of in school. This is how our society has been formed from the influences of celebrities, especially in the black community. It's more important for kids to know the names of different brands of clothes than for them to be worried about their studies. This is a good reason that uniforms should be worn in inner-city public schools.

In public schools, they only teach whatever is on

---

[17] http://www.greatschools.org/gk/articles/school-uniforms/

the standardized test. Whites who go to private and better public schools learn about more than just what's standard.[18] I'm sure there are some white kids who can tell you about stocks as if they were already working on Wall Street. Since 2000 to present, black students have a higher dropout rate than any other race.[19]

Teachers who are in poverty-stricken schools must know that they have to be a role model because of certain circumstances that children are in, from divorced homes to parents who do not care about their child's well-being. I believe that teachers should be approachable, because the trust of the adults in their home may be broken and the child may need help to better his or her situation.

School systems need to get the parents more involved and not solely rely on underpaid teachers. We should invite parents to help with fundraisers and field trips that they can go on with their child. I think communication is the breakdown between parents and schools. Schools that reside in the poorer areas of the city are terrible in comparison to the schools with good curriculum and activity structures. Some of these

---

[18] http://cepa.stanford.edu/content/private-school-racial-enrollments-and-segregation

[19] https://www.naacp.org/page/-/education%20documents/AfricanAmericansAndEducation.pdf

inner-city schools need attention that they are not receiving from the government. Delinquency affects those who are only the have-nots in life.

The deck is stacked against blacks, especially black men in America. The only thing you can do to change the way things are is to put yourself in the position to win. Blacks have to do more than getting college degrees. Being doctors, state attorneys, judges, politicians—either Republican or Democrat—these things matter and will help the process of being viewed inversely. You can change equality a little at a time until America can see that all black people aren't thugs who listen to rap music.

Chapter 7: The Importance of Voting

VOTING MATTERS—TO a degree. I think we can all agree that politicians don't do much for the people once elected. The only way that a politician does anything is if it's in their best interest. So what does that mean for black voices? They aren't being heard.

Black voices are not being heard because of the lack of follow-through within the black community. Blacks protest, but do not give adequate solutions to their problems. In order to receive the attention needed, we need to boycott stores peacefully. The black community protests for a few days, and then everyone goes back to their lives as if the issues will solve themselves.

Vote based on whom has the closest ideals or beliefs as you. I know that blacks mainly vote for Democrats, but some Democrats are not good and should not even be voted for. Just because politicians butter you up and tell blacks what they want to hear doesn't make it right to vote for them. The politicians understand that blacks have the potential to change the outcome of elections, so don't be fooled by the pandering of lying politicians. They don't care about the actual person behind the vote.

Many Republicans aren't worth voting for either, but if you're a business-minded person, some Republicans are better than Democrats. What about your neighborhoods? You should be voting for your city councilmen as well as other propositions that may benefit yourself and your community. Don't complain that nothing changes, especially if you didn't vote. Senators and congressmen do not have you, the voter, in mind, in my personal opinion.

Everyone needs to do his or her due diligence and check the backgrounds of those they are electing. In the 1980s, people could only go by what the politician would say. Now you can Google what they are saying and check their records for discrepancies. It's important that we not follow the crowd—we must form our *own* opinion. If someone votes one way, you should make your own decisions as an individual of the United States of America.

I think many blacks forget that it was only recently that we have been allowed to vote. In my opinion, not voting is the reason the black communities are in shambles. You have to vote for all elections. It's been about sixty years, and there are still people alive who weren't allowed to vote because they were black. Blacks were allowed to vote in 1870, which was a part of the fifteenth amendment. There were several states that did not allow for blacks to vote. Several states disregarded the fifteenth amendment. The voting rights act of 1965 was a law passed by President Lyndon Johnson, so that all blacks can vote regardless of what the state laws were at that time.[20] White America, do your homework and see that it hasn't been seventy years yet, and our anger is still fresh.

[21]http://godfatherpolitics.com/its-time-to-ban-the-democrat-party-the-party-of-slavery-and-jim-crow/

---

[20] https://www.loc.gov/rr/program/bib/ourdocs/15thamendment.html

[21]   http://godfatherpolitics.com/its-time-to-ban-the-democrat-party-the-party-of-slavery-and-jim-crow/

Chapter 8: The Current Culture of the Black Community

BLACK SPORTS FIGURES should be more boisterous when it comes to dealing with race and the unjust treatment of blacks in America. Interestingly, minority athletes make up the majority of the major sports played in the United States. That's a good opportunity for us to speak up.

But it doesn't stop at sports.

Rap music is a part of black culture like rednecks to country music. I know that America sees young black men getting money from telling their story of the hoods they came from. At times, the content of rap/hip-hop is a product of the environment in which the artist lives.

Rappers glorify the drug-dealing game, as if it were something to be proud of. I understand the struggle that blacks in the hood go through, since I was one of them. The misunderstanding comes from those who only judge blacks in a prejudiced light.

Whites only see blacks glorifying the horrid situations we face daily. Whites can come and steal our culture and take the pieces that they want of our culture.

Rap music is art that imitates the life of those around the rapper or his or her true stories. Rap has become an outlet to get blacks out of the ghettos, besides basketball and football. Should rappers be to blame for the way impressionable minds take their music? I would say yes and no—the parents should be in their children's lives.

Rappers who do have positive messages are hardly noticed by the general public. These rappers go unnoticed because their music isn't *street* enough with the words *nigga* and *bitch* as every other word. Mos Def, Common, and Immortal Technique are rappers who will not be recognized because they have uplifting messages in their music.

I think that the song "Moment of Clarity" by Jay Z shows that not the intellectual artist but the music industry disapproves due to record sales being more important.[22]

Truthfully, I wanna rhyme like Common Sense
But I did five mill'
I ain't been rhyming like Common since

Jay Z is stating that because of money, he will not rap to enlighten his audience because it would hurt his

---

[22] http://genius.com/Jay-z-moment-of-clarity-lyrics

fan base, which would ultimately hurt his cash flow. Jay Z goes on to say in another part of this verse:

We as rappers must decide what's most important
And I can't help the poor if I'm one of them
So I got rich and gave back
To me that's the win-win

Jay Z's influence on hip-hop was monumental. He is basically saying in this verse that he could rap as if he were to give knowledge to the people who listen to his music, but it wouldn't sell as many records. Jay Z gives back to his community, which is a win-win. The music industry doesn't have intellectual rappers because their music will not sell enough to make the music company's content.

If you see violence on a daily basis, it is more than likely you will think that this type of behavior is acceptable. This criminal behavior is a learned behavior. There are some kids who grow up with a silver spoon and still choose to make delinquent decisions. Some blacks do not have a choice but to be delinquent because of the circumstances they're in—circumstances that many youths are in could turn them into future criminals.

So even if you have to live in the ghetto, you can still clean up after yourself. Sweep the front area of your house and take pride in your home. If police are driving by in these ghettos and see the street you live on is filthy, this will make them think that those who live in these areas are filthy people and cannot understand why people would choose to live in those conditions.

There is little funding for the preservation of the inner cities that predominately house minorities. I can understand that some cities have turned their backs completely on any type of maintenance. There are city blocks in Philadelphia that are just abandoned buildings. These abandoned buildings are a haven for drug dealers and users to conduct criminal activities. Even with this happening, some blocks and houses that people live in are uninhabitable because of those who are receiving Section 8 housing. Some black Americans live in some very foul housing conditions because it is not their money that is paying for their rent.

As you can guess, the wealthy do not live in or near these crime-infested areas. People with subsidized housing are all assembled together, which eventually makes them potential criminals. This makes it hard for many minorities to believe that there is a way out of their terrible situation.

The TV show *Empire* is an underling reinforcement that again displays blacks in a thug mentality. And of course, America is in love with this TV show. The fact is, *Empire* is exploiting black America and is definitely destroying the little foundation that blacks have to represent themselves in a positive nature. *Empire* shows the violence of the hood and the struggles that black America does go through to try to get the American dream. It is a good TV show if you're blindly degrading your own race.

Besides television adding to stereotyping, white people tend to look down on blacks who wear designer brands or walk into high-dollar stores. Because of profiling, whites think blacks are going to steal from the store or rob them.

Some rappers can be seen wearing Gucci, Louis Vuitton, and many other popular name brands. Blacks, as a race that influences the nation, should be making their own brands and supporting one another. But black-owned businesses and establishments are hard to find. So when you find them, support them!

Nicki Minaj has very affordable clothing with the stylish looks that she wears herself. Her clothing line is available at Sears.

Then there is Kanye West clothing and shoes known as Yeezy. Sadly, Kanye's clothing is very expensive. Maybe you've seen the photo of a purposely ripped Yeezy sweater being sold for $2,500 in a retail store.

White America sees blacks on YouTube videos and takes from the culture when it benefits themselves. Whites have hijacked black Americans' style and music for a long time.

If you watch TV, many commercials are directed to specific audiences, but they use black culture words or music to catch the audience. Black culture is sprinkled everywhere, yet there are still many inequalities.

With all this stereotyping, it's time blacks give society a better outlook on how we are depicted. Blacks need to give the public something else to think about so that we can shake the systematic cycle of profiling and oppression.

Reality TV shows like the *Housewives of Atlanta* have black women who act like they're still in the poverty-stricken neighborhoods that they were raised in. Why? They have money and Birkin bags, so why are they on TV fighting? And if you've ever watched an episode, you know I don't mean talking negatively about one another. America is watching these women throw punches at each other. Yet blacks want white America to accept them for who they are, even though they see you acting like hoodlums. Black females should be setting the path that other black females can follow.

Your story is simple: you made it out of the hood and young black girls can make it too without degrading themselves.

We know that's not what we are seeing on TV. It's another chance to change how people in America perceive blacks.

That's what they're getting paid for: conflicts amongst the group. In the overall light, these people make blacks look bad for money.

And that's the sad reality of these reality shows.

But it doesn't stop there. We need sports figures

to become better role models too. I get it: you didn't have a dad, but you can still act like men and carry yourselves as so. There are too many football players who are constantly in trouble for stupid things like weed and DUIs. If you're making that kind of money, then set the example and call for an Uber.

Muhammad Ali was a controversial role model who took on issues that blacks still deal with today. Ali dressed well, told the truth, and gave hope to many that you can make it out of your awful situation with hard work and dedication. Sports figures need to become a helping hand to those in the hood. They need to voice their thoughts on black-on-black crime. There was a time when black athletes spoke out on civil rights.

At the present time, it seems as if they are more worried about their checks or are afraid of losing sponsors.

I know for sure that blacks need to pull together and start fixing how they handle life. If blacks valued life like they valued their Jordans, then blacks would not be killing each other over property that doesn't belong to them in the first place. Gangs are taking over Chicago, Los Angeles, and many other major cities in America because of this mentality.

The young gangster who thinks it's cool to show his guns in videos: cut that out. You make it easy for police to arrest you and to prosecute. When you go to court and your character is being questioned, you'll regret trying to look cool on Vine or Instagram.

If you did the crime, man up to what you did and stop being scared of the consequences. If you are scared of the consequences, don't be in the streets doing things that can get you incarcerated. I know snitching is frowned upon in the black community, but we have to fight this stigmatism to get our neighborhoods back from criminals.

There are many people who are afraid to speak out about those who commit serious crimes. If you know that a killer is living on your street or next door and you're terrified to mention it to the police, then realize that there are ways to notify the police anonymously and you won't be labeled as a snitch. If you're a person doing criminal activities and you don't want to go to jail, then find another profession.

You know that old saying, "Don't do the crime if you can't do the time."

If you know someone did a serious crime and you chose not to notify the police, you're just as guilty as the person who committed the crime.

Another thing I don't get is the looting of businesses in your community. Just because they overcharge for stuff doesn't mean you burn it down.

Protest peacefully instead.

It doesn't make sense to burn down stores in your own neighborhood—a black neighborhood at that! I have personally never seen white people protest and burn down anything. There has to be a point when blacks have to take responsibility for their actions and stop putting blame on everything and everyone else.

The situations that you can control? Take *complete* control and make a path for yourself and others to follow.

Chapter 9: Nigga vs. Black

YOU ARE NOT going to die from someone saying the word *nigga*. It is a slave mentality to keep grasping on to a word that many of us haven't really endured. I think we have to move on from a word that has so many negative feelings behind the meaning. If we stop saying it in every rap song, it will fade away.

But to my grandma, that word means something completely different. Blacks don't want whites to say it, but many songs have the word *nigga* in them. We all know white kids love rap/hip-hop music so they say *nigga* all the time in their rooms or their cars. They probably do not know the actual root meaning of the word *nigga*. To many black Americans, they believe that *nigga* shouldn't be said at all in any context. I can understand the reason behind this thought, but it's going to take time before people realize that the word *nigga*, no matter the context, shouldn't be said ever.

If someone says *nigga* in a degrading way, just say, "Thank you for noticing," and keep moving.

When you entertain these racist people, it gives them the reaction they want. They want to get under your skin. They want to rattle you so you get angry and lash out. Then they can call the cops. Then you're the one who looks like an animal when you're going to jail, so don't give them that satisfaction. We must let go of the slave-like ideals to become better. If we don't, we will never surpass the actions of those who enslaved blacks for hundreds of years.

We as blacks in America have been wearing chains for so long that it is programmed in our heads for it to be normal to go jail. I'm tired of seeing blacks going to prison for things that they are capable of changing. It bothers me to my very soul to see that some blacks *want* to be enslaved.

The slaves had no choice but to wear shackles around their hands, neck, and feet their entire lives, wanting, *praying* to be free. In these days, blacks are giving up their freedom that many take for granted. We are a disgrace to those who died for our civil rights. Many died because they looked at their so-called master incorrectly. Slaves were told they looked like monkeys. For pure fun, slave masters liked to kill a nigger because they were bored. Slaves died thinking their name was *nigger*. Slaves died not knowing what freedom was, not being able to go to school or read. Slaves didn't have families and those who did have families were separated and sold to the highest bidder. Think about that when you say the word *nigga*!

We are enslaved to ourselves. Blacks expect handouts instead of a hand up, relying on their EBT cards. I remember when being on welfare wasn't cool. Now it is acceptable, which is pathetic and disgraceful. We need to have some dignity. If a slave were alive to see the world we live in, they would be ashamed and I don't blame them for feeling that way.

I was once told by a wise man that there is a difference between a "nigga" and being a "black man/woman." I was a teen when he told me that "a black man gets up for work and makes sure his family is taken care of no matter the situation. If a black man has to work from sun up to sun down and the graveyard shift, he'll do it if necessary." There aren't many men who even consider working, let alone putting his family before himself.

A nigga will hustle, lie, steal, but will cry to the police when shit hits the fan. Niggas will loot their own neighborhood stores without thinking. Niggas will rob the corner store when they need money and go to the same store and buy something the next day. A nigga will kill another nigga over getting shorted on a twenty-dollar bag of weed. Niggas will kill you for ten dollars over a dice game. Niggas will buy themselves clothes for the weekend but won't pay child support or take care of their children. *Niggas* are what white America is seeing. They can't distinguish from niggas and blacks. The blacks are people who do right by society.

I'm sure some people have called me a coon, which I couldn't care less about because my family has always had what they needed. Listen, what they *needed*, not what they *wanted*. There is a difference between the two. You need a house, electricity, and food. You want Jordans and PlayStation games and name-brand clothes. I had to work minimum-wage jobs to get by, and it wasn't easy. I, the man of the house, did what I had to do as a man to take care of my family.

Young niggas do not respect their elders. When I was growing up, that was the number-one thing I was taught: to respect your elders and don't talk back. "Be seen, not heard," was what I was told. Somehow, that has gotten lost with the behavior of black youth. Why is it that I see black kids fighting with their elders on a city bus or train? It makes no sense. And then they end up on WordStar thinking it's cool. It's not! Ask yourself, "What do I get from fighting an old man or woman who can't defend him or herself?" And yet, you want America to see blacks in a different light? Niggas young and old cannot see the damage they are causing by acting like damn fools. This is how America is constantly picturing blacks in general.

Black women always complain that they can't find a good man. I'll tell you why: you find this guy on the block or the club and expect for him to change for you. Black women on Instagram, Facebook, and

Twitter are damn near naked and twerking on Vine. Nothing about that is classy. I know that all black women do not act in this manner. For those black women who do act like this, just think, black people aren't the only ones with the know-how of social media. Your actions make the black women who are trying to do better for themselves look like shit. The women who are doing slut-like activities on social media are setting a horrible example for other impressionable young black girls.

There are many black fathers who support their child by paying child support, but they have a crazy baby mama so they can't ever see their child. She has so much hatred toward the father for no real reason. The father pays child support on time, but his child doesn't have food or school supplies that he or she needs. The baby mama has a new weave, her nails done, and new weekend gear so she can step out to the club. They should make child support payments traceable so that the father can see where his money is going. Niggas using child support to support themselves is a broke, discreditable hustle. Provide for yourself and your family, and stop waiting for your baby daddy to come save you with your child's child support payment.

How is it that black people in the hood have the same clothes that the white kids have in the suburbs? If you have Jordans with no food in your house, you might need to reevaluate your life in its entirety. You should be using that money to get your child to a better house, in a better neighborhood so that your child can go to a better public school.

As a black man born and raised in America, I can tell the difference between niggas and blacks, but the rest of the world cannot distinguish the difference. There are a lot of niggas who make us, black Americans who are working hard to get ahead in life, look really bad.

Chapter 10: Learn to Invest

I LEARNED A lot of money management on my own. I didn't understand what a credit score was or how to use it. I had used my credit to get my first cell phone and credit card. No one told me that having good credit is ideal to making bigger purchases in the future, like a house and car.

I will break it down as simple as I can just to give you a little insight on how to use your credit. Your credit line is very important because it can determine how much a creditor will lend.

Many young blacks may not understand the power of their credit line. If you have bad credit, you probably already understand that your credit is important. Someone with good credit can purchase a car or house or get a credit card with a low interest rate. If you have bad credit, your interest rate will be very high and will limit your purchasing power.

I personally do not pay for items unless I'm using cash. If I cannot pay cash, I will not buy or purchase the item. When I'm looking to buy furniture or a TV, I use cash. If I'm purchasing a car or house, that is when I would use my credit. If you can't afford to buy small things in cash, do not buy it, because you will end up paying more for the product you purchased than what it is worth. Places like Rent-A-Center and Aaron's are not good deals. It looks like a good deal, but with all the hidden charges and interest, you will pay more for furniture that you could have saved up for something else.

Check-cashing places are a scam. They take a high percentage of your check and expect you to come back again. Most banks accounts are free to set up, so why pay extra money at the check-cashing place only to wind up with less money? The fact is that many of you don't know any better because you see others do it so you do it as well. This is wrong. Learn how to open a bank account for free. I also think that many Americans use check-cashing places because they are lazy and do not want to bother dealing with a free bank account. If you have time to keep up with the Kardashians, then you should have time to find out things to improve yourself.

If you are a parent and you have used your child's credit, please don't leave your teenage child with your careless debt. I understand times do get hard, but you are having your child start their adult life with bad credit. Those with bad credit know how hard it is to get their credit score back up to a respectable level.

If you're trying to get your credit back on track,

first find out what you owe and who you owe the money to. Then I would start paying them off one by one until your debt is cleared. Once your debt is cleared, it may take at least a year from the time you paid off a debt to see your credit begin to rise. You can also speak with a financial adviser and they can give you better advice on how to approach your specific situation.

Black people have no idea what Wall Street is or what really happens on Wall Street. If you're a real hustler, that is where you should be, and you don't need your traditional education to buy stocks anymore. Blacks need to wake up and watch how white folks move and how they are getting their money.[23] Again, that's money you could use to actually get ahead. It isn't easy and if it were easy, it wouldn't be America.

Always remember if you conduct yourself like a man or woman, you can easily change the outcome of the future. You can make the future that you want for yourself and your family. Try not to contemplate too far ahead. Don't think five years ahead. Think about what you can do *today* to better yourself so that you can accomplish your short-term goals.

An example of short-term goals would be: you need to study for a test tomorrow, so by studying for this test, you can get a good score. In turn, this gives

---

[23] http://www.businessinsider.com/wall-street-bank-diversity-2015-8

you a higher grade point average. A good GPA can possibly get you a scholarship to a respectable college. I put my personal goals on a list so that I'm able to read them to ensure that I'm doing them on a day-by-day basis. I do this because it makes it easier to accomplish. Remember: don't make your goals so farfetched that you don't actually believe them yourself.

This is a good way to make money: save a couple dollars from your income tax check and invest it into stocks or bonds. I personally would shop around for stocks or bonds that would best fit your interest. It's always good to have more than one stream of income.

Saving money is good, but you need to have an idea of what to do with it after you've saved so much, like stocks or buying a rental property. You can buy a rental property and rent it to someone and make a good cash flow along with your job. The white folks are leaps and bounds ahead of us on how to make money more than one way. Always remember they can't take what you own, in theory.

In 1921, there were wealthy blacks in Tulsa, Oklahoma. At that time, it was called Black Wall Street.[24] The reason it was called Black Wall Street was because of a community of blacks who were prospering. There were black-owned hospitals and

---

[24] http://www.pbs.org/wnet/jimcrow/stories_events_tulsa.html

stores. As we all know, this ended in jealousy from white America. Black Wall Street eventually was frowned upon by those who hated blacks the most: the KKK. So at one point in time, blacks owned something and it was taken away yet again by white America. How many white Americans know about Black Wall Street? They should know how they destroyed the dreams of many blacks Americans in Tulsa. It's saying there was a black community that worked together to put themselves in a better position in life, then it can be done again if we cooperate with one another.

The Black Wall Street story is tragic, but the good in the story is that it is possible to organize and work together as a united black community.

Chapter 11: Movements

CONTRARY TO POPULAR belief, the Black Lives Matter movement is not a terrible thing. There are some things I would like for this movement to accomplish. Mainly being more involved in the major cities of crime like Chicago, Baltimore, and Philadelphia. Black violence should matter as well. Blacks need to start Black on Black Lives Matter. I want Black Lives Matter (BLM) to be protesting and causing havoc for all blacks who are being killed by each other in each major city. BLM shows up only when a white cop has killed another black man. Only getting into an uproar when white police officers kill black men is illogical. Blacks kill more blacks than police. Blacks who die by the hands of black crimes is 52 percent, which is higher than any other race.[25] I understand that police should not be killing anyone

---

[25]   https://ucr.fbi.gov/crime-in-the-u.s/2013/crime-in-the-u.s.-2013/tables/table-43

who is unarmed and defenseless. But if you want white America to take the movement seriously, then you have to begin within the black community.

BLM needs a strong representative like Dr. Martin Luther King Jr. Depending on who is being interviewed, the message can be conflicted between different speakers. BLM has to speak up for those who are killed due to gang violence and black-on-black crime in general. Individually, we can't beat this system, but together, it is possible.

The movement Black on Black Lives Matter would be a just cause to stop the unnecessary violence in all cities that are predominantly black. If this movement were functioning, I would make the communities better and safer for everyone involved. In these communities, blacks can open up recreation centers to give those black children somewhere to go instead of standing outside on the corner. The community can help by clearing vacant lots to make basketball courts or playgrounds.

Blacks, we have to stop killing each other over nothing. If there were more men to be actual fathers in black communities, many things would have different outcomes. A better lifestyle, and many families could afford to move themselves out of poverty into the middle class. A black middle-class family then can give an example to those who are still in poverty. If blacks were to look at other ethnicities, they could see how other ethnicities work to help each other. Other ethnicities work together more than blacks. We are always in our own way—since the 1980s, starting with the drugs flowing through our communities. Even today, we are tripping over ourselves so that we can't get ahead.

In these major cities, like Philadelphia and Chicago, cops don't kill as many black men compared to black-on-black crime. Why isn't BLM standing in Chicago blocking the gangs from shooting and killing each other? Black-on-black crime should matter.

In 2015, there were 468 murders in one year from gun violence.[26] There were 2,900 shootings in Chicago in 2015. It is unbelievable that this occurs in the US at this high of a rate. If these shootings were occurring in white communities, it would be called an epidemic. Chicago had 7,000 guns that were taken off the streets by police in the past year. Gun control laws will not stop criminals from getting guns.

Black America, if you want to change something, you have to start with *us* first. We can't change America's view of blacks until everyone looks in the mirror.

Once we as a black community have looked at ourselves in the mirror, we can adjust what is needed accordingly. We have to fix the problems in the black community, and then blacks can proceed with forward

---

[26] http://time.com/4165576/chicago-murders-shootings-rise-2015/

progress. Black America can go with a smile and tell America, we fixed the problems at home, so let's get this hatred fixed amongst all nationalities. After this, we can then be heard and taken more seriously.

Chapter 12: Internalized Racism

IF YOU ARE a black person but a different shade of black, that person is known as yellow skinned, even though they are still black. The technical term for this is called *colorism*.[27] The dark-skinned person is jealous or vice versa. This form of black-on-black hostility is an extremely ugly form of racism. Being jealous of each other, which are both black, is pretty dumb. You need to be happy that you're dark or yellow.

I hate when blacks attack other blacks who have made it out of poverty. Let's take Don Lemon, host of *CNN Tonight*, for example. I don't think I have heard any black person that I know say anything nice about the man. You should be trying to figure out what he did to be where he is instead of calling him an Uncle Tom. I understand that those in positions like Don

---

[27] http://www.merriam-webster.com/dictionary/colorism

Lemon do need to speak up on behalf of black America. Steven A. Smith from ESPN always speaks on behalf of blacks regardless of the situation.

Black Americans are constantly dealing with racism. We deal with racism on a daily basis. Yet we profile each other. I do profile other blacks sometimes and I know I'm not the only one. I had seen a black man in a nice car, and the first thing that came to mind was, "Is he a hustler?" He could have been a doctor for all I knew. I'm wrong for that way of thinking, but it has been a part of black Americans to profile each other because the division that whites want to occur. Blacks need to stop constantly profiling each other and help each other get ahead in life.

Most African-Americans don't even truly know if they are from African descent. Many blacks talk as if they are African-American. I often wonder, *What part of Africa are you from?* Most don't know or care enough to find out.

Africans I have spoken to do not want to be associated with black Americans. I believe this is because we are a humiliation to true African-Americans. If you know where you're from, you can say, "I'm African-American." Some of you might be from Jamaica or some other island where dark-skinned people reside. So let's all be more aware of what is going on around us before we speak out on something we may not know about. With that being said, you are black and you live in the US, so that is the card you were dealt.

Being white has become a *thing*. There are a lot of blacks who are bleaching their skin to become more white.[28] This is vile to change your skin to fit in with a different race. We need to be stronger than this. We need to value our beautiful skin color.

People in the hood still give shit to black people who are in good public schools and have parent(s) who do not live in poverty. I have heard people say, "You talk white." I talk white because I can pronounce my words clearly and intelligently. I shouldn't have to dumb down my words because you don't read a book or don't have an education past the tenth grade. The sad thing is, while in high school, I had to dumb down my thoughts so people could understand the words I was saying. I don't understand why blacks get mad because they don't know the words you're using. Then they will call you uppity. It is sad that rappers had to dumb down their music because niggas aren't smart enough to figure out or know what the message is that they are trying to get across.

---

[28] http://www.huffingtonpost.com/news/skin-lightening/

Chapter 13: Purposely Divided

PLAYING THE RACE card is a situation in its own right. Should we as blacks keep using the race card? There are times to use the race card and times not to. It's a hard thing to use the race card, but if you have to use it, then make sure it's for a good reason. If we want to get along with white folks, I consider we put the race card in our back pocket until needed. Like insurance, you only use it when you need it.

Why is it that white folks are scared of blacks? Many white folks do not interact with blacks enough to know about us, but they're scared of us. America is made for whites. *I'm* the one who is scared to walk out of my house in my own neighborhood. If I were to walk around in Cherry Hill, New Jersey, I'm going to attract the attention of the police and all I'm doing is walking to work. Yet, white folks are scared.

Another thing America needs to get on board with is to stop with the ethnic questions on applications and surveys: Black, Hispanic, Asian, White, African-American, and what other race you can squeeze into that little box. This is a subliminal divide. It's like stating, "Hey, don't forget you're black or Latino," as if I didn't know. Is it necessary for everybody to know the breakdown of races? There are times that statistics do need to be recorded to inform the public. I don't believe it is necessary in many cases to have race on things that don't report statistics, and needs to be stopped.

White America wonders why there is a divide in the country. I know that blacks were supposed to get forty acres and a mule. America was literally built on the backs of African slaves, and we still have nothing to show for hundreds of years of oppression.

Yet we aren't smart enough to take advantage of the situation.

I know times are hard, but if you never try to find a job or create one, then you're just waiting on your EBT or SNAP card payment to come through. This is what niggas still haven't figured out: if you do nothing, you get nothing. The little money you get and wait on is still coming from the same government that makes money by oppressing the black community.

Niggas, you are poor so you're out in the streets trappin' and you get put in the judicial system. The government gets money from taxpayers to keep blacks locked up behind bars. This is a cycle that goes around and around. For the most part, you haven't caught on to what's happening around you. If you read or watched the news, you would see how blacks are being portrayed and maybe that would change your actions, but most won't do that.

Blacks can't keep playing the victim anymore. There are ways to get what you want if you apply yourself to your cause. There are scholarships that blacks can get for just being black. You can go to college and get grants that you do not ever have to pay back. It's up to you as a black man or woman to find out how to get the resources you need to get ahead in life.

A minority of whites would love for blacks to go back to Africa or whatever other country blacks came from originally. So if the world were without blacks, what would be the outcome and how would the world look? I think this is a conversation that probably happens behind closed doors. The difference is that black America tells you directly our issues, but it falls upon deaf ears.

The world would have less culture without black people. Blacks are doctors, lawyers, priests, ministers, teachers, astronauts, musicians, scientists, and mathematicians. African art wouldn't have existed. We would not only be missing the majority of a large continent, but we'd be missing a huge population on other continents. As we all know, blacks have left a huge imprint on sports. Imagine basketball without Michael Jordan. There would be no black Americans. A world without black people would probably be a world where America took a lot longer to build without black slaves.

Hollywood has always had roles for other races besides whites. There have been white Indians and white black people who have won awards for portraying other races. The moment someone suggests a black man to be James Bond or a Storm Trooper, people flip out. It's okay that Hollywood has white-washed everything, especially the roles of minority ethnicities.

There are some things blacks must do to be equals. I believe blacks need to act in better movies to get the accolades they deserve. The movie *Chi-Raq* was a good start to begin the healing process that America has to go through to begin peace. The movie *Selma* was great acting and to not have won an Oscar is inexplicable, to say the least. In my opinion, the movie *Dope* was worthy to be at least nominated. It explains life as a black youth in an inner city that gets mixed up with the wrong people. It had great acting and a good plot but no awards.

Blacks get butt hurt when they aren't nominated for awards that are predominately for white people. Blacks have BET and the NAACP awards. There aren't whites getting nominated for those awards, just like the Oscars. We can't have it both ways. Blacks are either going to be united or divided. I think united is better to ease the tension between the races. I do understand that blacks should still have been nominated for the roles that were stellar.

The Jim Crow effect is alive and well. Everything that I have spoken on has to do with the Jim Crow effect. In our society, whites are just now seeing the effects of hundreds of years of slavery and what it has done to America as a whole. Separate but equal doesn't exist in America. "I look to a day when people will not be judged by the color of their skin, but by the content of their character."[29] Dr. Martin Luther King Jr. said this in the 1960s and it still hasn't come to fruition completely.

After the American Civil War (1861–1865), most southern states and border states passed laws that denied blacks basic human rights. Jim Crow became a kind of shorthand for the laws, customs, and etiquette that segregated and demeaned black Americans primarily from the 1870s to the 1960s.[30]

So even after the Civil War, blacks were still treated like slaves, even though slavery was abolished in 1865. It wasn't until 1965 that blacks began to be treated better than slaves. It took one hundred years after slavery was abolished to get treated as fairly as whites would allow. Not much has changed since 1965 for blacks. We still get treated like second-rate citizens at best.

---

[29] https://www.archives.gov/press/exhibits/dream-speech.pdf

[30] http://www.ferris.edu/jimcrow/origins.htm

There were times that blacks couldn't join the military. Then when blacks were allowed to join the military, it was still segregated, which is stupid in theory. I can fight for the country I live and die in, but I can't get a drink out of the same water fountain as the white folks. "Go around back, nigger," is what they said back in a time of segregation. Many white Americans don't care about anything that doesn't affect them.

Affirmative action is positive efforts to recruit minority group members or women for jobs, promotions, and educational opportunities. No affirmative action has been in place since the 1960s,[31] but the workforce only hired black men as a token black guy to avoid any lawsuits. As the token black guy, your wages still wouldn't be that of the white woman who worked in the same field.[32][33] Blacks knowingly worked even though white women were being paid more, which is upsetting not because they

---

[31]

http://www.civilrights.org/resources/civilrights101/affirmaction.html?ref errer=https://www.google.com/

[32]   https://www.washingtonpost.com/news/wonk/wp/2013/08/28/these-seven-charts-show-the-black-white-economic-gap-hasnt-budged-in-50-years/

were white but because they were doing the same job—thus, no equality. It has just started getting better for blacks in the 1960s and pretty much stayed there since. We as a society have not progressed as a people and we are not all to blame.

The South Carolina Confederate Flag debate that occurred in 2015 was ridiculous. How does America expect for blacks to react when you are constantly reminded about slavery by the state flag? The fact that there are flags in the US that still have the Confederate Flag symbol is repulsive. The confederate flags should not have ever been flown as a part of state flags after the Civil War. The designer of the flag, William Tappan Thompson, said, "As a people, we are fighting to maintain the heaven-ordained supremacy of the white man over the inferior or colored races. A White Flag would be thus emblematical of our cause." He dubbed the new flag "the White Man's Flag.[34]

White America needs to think about the flag situation like this: if there were a bully at your school and he beat you up every day, then this bully has a flag flown in your living room, you will never forget or move on from that bully as long as that flag is in your living room.

---

[34]

https://en.wikipedia.org/wiki/Flags_of_the_Confederate_States_of_America

The culture of violence in America has permeated the white American psyche. White America came to this country and repossessed land that didn't belong to the settlers. America from the very beginning started off on the wrong foot. Whites butchered the Native Americans. Then they enslaved Africans. The African slaves built this country. Then whites built churches on stolen land and proclaimed "In God We Trust."

The sad truth is, America was built on violence.

Final Thoughts

I AM NOT an ideal role model, but if someone needs help, I'm for helping someone out. I'm not trying to put anyone down. Don't take what I'm saying out of the context in which I wrote it. I know we, as a society, can do better. Blacks have put each other down long enough.

So the overall solution would be to start over. Find a time machine, go back in time, and change what happened several hundred years ago. Until an actual time machine is invented, we, as a society, need to find a way to get along. Blacks, whites, Asians, and Latinos need to work together to defeat the underlying segregation that is poisoning our society. The true meaning of *freedom* is equal opportunity on the basis of ability that is presented to yourself. The fact that you are in America gives you a better chance to survive compared to other countries where there is no such thing as *freedom*!

I would like for whites to think of blacks in a better way to avoid awkward encounters. If blacks were on their A game, it would make it easier for everyone to get along with each other. If blacks were more about getting better jobs and having their own money, it would cause whites to look at blacks differently. So that the white lady walking down the street knows I can afford whatever is in her purse, so there is no need for her to clutch it as I walk past her or as she crosses the street, as if I were a ravenous dog with rabies.

Blacks also need to change within our communities so that we can be taken seriously. Blacks have to get the family dynamic back to help the success of your family's best outcome. There will never be a politician that will listen to our complaints and genuinely care. Blacks have every reason to be mad about what is occurring in our great nation. Some whites want blacks to separate themselves from them so that they can have their own country.

There can't be only one person to change the current conditions of black society. I know if blacks united, that together change can happen. There will always be those who will struggle within the black community, with the thought of change. Like any reorganization, there is always those who rebel, but eventually, they too will have to get on board.

The question is, does white America want change? Does black America want change? We have to be honest with ourselves for change to transpire. I do want America to change for me and my family as well as yours! Until death do us part, America. Black Americans aren't going anywhere, so let's get this counseling together and progress forward as a United Nation.

As for Black America, you are not chained like slaves. Most blacks can read and we do speak English. You can't tell me that you have no choice. You have a better chance than the generations before us. The cycle for change has to start now!

Acknowledgments

I WOULD LIKE to thank my family for giving me the courage to express myself through the writing of this book. I would not have finished this book if my Uncle Tony had not given me the push I needed to complete this process.

I would like to thank my closest friends for their motivation to keep me going when I felt defeated. Alexander and Jason are the reason that I decided to really put my thoughts on paper. We all had similar feelings on how society is today.

Finally, to my loving and supportive wife, Dia. She was able to give great relief to recognize that you were willing to provide and maintain the stability of the house as I completed my effort in this book.

Thank you all for your support. It is sincerely appreciated.

References

Association, T. P. (2008). *Reduce Class Sizes*. Retrieved from The Pennsylvania State Education Association r: https://www.psea.org/uploadedFiles/LegislationAndPolitics/Vision/Vision_ReduceClassSizes.pdf

Blackdemographics. (2014). *Households*. Retrieved from Blackdemographics: http://blackdemographics.com/households/poverty/

Congress, L. o. (2016). *Primary Documents in American History*. Retrieved from Libaray of Congress : https://www.loc.gov/rr/program/bib/ourdocs/15thamendment.html

Cook, L. (2015). *U.S. Education: Still Separate and Unequal*. Retrieved from US News: http://www.usnews.com/news/blogs/data-mine/2015/01/28/us-education-still-separate-and-unequal

Coski, J. (2016). *Flags of the Confederate States of America*. Retrieved from Wikipedia: https://en.wikipedia.org/wiki/Flags_of_the_Confederate_States_of_America

D'Antuono, M. (2012). *A Tale of Hoodies*. Retrieved from Abagond World Press:

https://abagond.wordpress.com/2012/04/24/michael-dantuono-a-tale-of-two-hoodies/

Darling-Hammond, L. (1998). *Unequal Opportunity: Race and Education*. Retrieved from Brookings.edu: http://www.brookings.edu/research/articles/1998/03/spring-education-darling-hammond

Davids, L. (2016). *Skin Lightening*. Retrieved from Huffingtonpost: http://www.huffingtonpost.com/news/skin-lightening/

FBI. (2013). *Crime in the United States 2013*. Retrieved from FBI UCR: https://ucr.fbi.gov/crime-in-the-u.s/2013/crime-in-the-u.s.-2013/tables/table-43

Ferris. (2015). *Jim Crow Museum*. Retrieved from Ferris State University: http://www.ferris.edu/jimcrow/origins.htm

Gao, G. (2014). *Chart of the Week: The black-white gap in incarceration rates*. Retrieved from Pew Research Center: http://www.pewresearch.org/fact-tank/2014/07/18/chart-of-the-week-the-black-white-gap-in-incarceration-rates/

Gavett, G. (2012, July). *Timeline: 30 Years of AIDS in Black America*. Retrieved from pbs.org: http://www.pbs.org/wgbh/frontline/article/timeline-30-years-of-aids-in-black-america/

Goodnough, A. (2000). *On Teacher Pay, City vs. Suburbs isn't that Simple*. Retrieved from New York Times: http://www.nytimes.com/2000/05/31/nyregion/on-teacher-pay-city-vs-suburbs-isn-t-that-simple.html

Hendley, M. (2014). *Racism Accusations in Shanesha Taylor Case Based on Inaccurate Information*. Retrieved from Phoenix New Times: http://www.phoenixnewtimes.com/news/racism-accusations-in-shanesha-taylor-case-based-on-inaccurate-information-6658545

Inazu, J. (2014). *Are We Ferguson?* Retrieved from CNN: http://www.cnn.com/2014/08/21/opinion/inazu-ferguson-race-class-brown/

Kerby, S. (2012). *The Top 10 Most Startling Facts About People of Color and Criminal Justice in the United States*. Retrieved from American Progress: https://www.americanprogress.org/issues/race/news/2012/03/13/11351/the-top-10-most-startling-facts-about-people-of-color-and-criminal-justice-in-the-united-states/

King, D. L. (1963). *I Have a Dream archives*. Retrieved from Archives.gov: https://www.archives.gov/press/exhibits/dream-speech.pdf

Long, H. (n.d.). *America's economic sore spot: Do black jobs matter?* Retrieved from http://money.cnn.com/2015/11/12/news/economy/black-jobs-matter/: http://money.cnn.com/2015/11/12/news/economy/black-jobs-matter/

Meghan Keneally, J. H. (2014, December).

Cleveland Cops 'Recklessly' Shot Boy, 12, Over Toy Gun, Suit Claims. Retrieved from ABC News: http://abcnews.go.com/US/cleveland-cops-recklessly-shot-boy-12-toy-gun/story?id=27402837

Merriam-Webster. (2015). *Colorism*. Retrieved from Merriam-Webster: http://www.merriam-webster.com/dictionary/colorism

Merriam-Webster. (2016). *Nigger*. Retrieved from Merriam-Webster: http://www.merriam-webster.com/dictionary/nigger

Michael Winter. (2014). *KKK membership sinks 2 Florida cops*. Retrieved from Usa Today: http://www.usatoday.com/story/news/nation/2014/07/14/florid-police-kkk/12645555/

Monitor, G. M. (2012). *Chart of the day: US Manufacturing Employmen*. Retrieved from Credit Write Downs: https://www.creditwritedowns.com/2012/05/chart-of-the-day-us-manufacturing-unemployment-1960-2012.html

NAACP. (2008). *CRIMINAL JUSTICE FACT SHEET*. Retrieved from NAACP: http://www.naacp.org/pages/criminal-justice-fact-sheet

NAACP. (2009). *African American and Education*. Retrieved from NAACP: https://www.naacp.org/page/-/education%20documents/AfricanAmericansAndEducation.pdf

Neibergal, C. (2012). *Students of Color Still Receiving Unequal Education*. Retrieved from American Progress: https://www.americanprogress.org/issues/education/news/2012/08/22/32862/students-of-color-still-receiving-unequal-education/

Plumer, B. (2013). *These ten charts show the black-white economic gap hasn't budged in 50 years*. Retrieved from Wahington Post: https://www.washingtonpost.com/news/wonk/wp/2013/08/28/these-seven-charts-show-the-black-white-economic-gap-hasnt-budged-in-50-years/

Portia Crowe, A. K. (2015, August). *These charts show just how white and male Wall Street really is*. Retrieved from Bussiness Insider: http://www.businessinsider.com/wall-street-bank-diversity-2015-8

Prevention, C. f. (2015). *Health of Black or African American non-Hispanic Population*. Retrieved from CDC: http://www.cdc.gov/nchs/fastats/black-health.htm

Sanburn, J. (2015). *Chicago Shootings and Murders Surged in 2015*. Retrieved from TIME: http://time.com/4165576/chicago-murders-shootings-rise-2015/

Sean F. Reardon, J. T. (2002). *Private school racial enrollments and segregation*. Retrieved from Stanford Cepa: http://cepa.stanford.edu/content/private-school-racial-enrollments-and-segregation

Services, H. (2016). *Trends in Teens*. Retrieved from Health&Human Services: http://www.hhs.gov/ash/oah/adolescent-health-topics/reproductive-health/teen-pregnancy/trends.html

Soffen, K. (2016). *The big question about why police pull over so many black drivers*. Retrieved from Washington Post: https://www.washingtonpost.com/news/wonk/wp/2016/07/08/the-big-question-about-why-police-pull-over-so-many-black-drivers/

Sparks, S. D. (2011, August). *Study Finds Metal Detectors More Common in High-Minority Schools*. Retrieved from Education Week: http://www.edweek.org/ew/articles/2011/08/31/02security.h31.html

Statistics, B. o. (2013). *Marriage and divorce: patterns by gender, race, and educational attainment*. Retrieved from Bureau of Labor Statistics: http://www.bls.gov/opub/mlr/2013/article/marriage-and-divorce-patterns-by-gender-race-and-educational-attainment.htm

Ventura, S. J. (n.d.). *National and State Patterns of Teen Births in the*. Retrieved from Center of Disease Control and Prevention: http://www.cdc.gov/nchs/data/nvsr/nvsr63/nvsr63_04.pdf

Violence., M. P. (2016). *Mapping Police Violence*. Retrieved from Mapping Police Violence.:

http://mappingpoliceviolence.org/unarmed/

Wallace, G. (2015, January). *Only 5 black CEOs at 500 biggest companies*. Retrieved from cnnmoney. com:

http://money.cnn.com/2015/01/29/news/economy/mcd onalds-ceo-diversity/

Walsh, M. (2014, October). *Florida man gets life in prison for killing teen over loud music*. Retrieved from Ny Daily News:

http://www.nydailynews.com/news/crime/florida-man-life-prison-killing-teen-loud-music-article-1.1978021

Watch, H. R. (2008). *Targeting Blacks Drug Law Enforcement and Race in the United States*. Retrieved from hrw.org:

https://www.hrw.org/sites/default/files/reports/us0508 _1.pdf

Wilde, M. (2016). *Do uniforms make schools better*. Retrieved from Great Schools:

http://www.greatschools.org/gk/articles/school-uniforms/

Wormser, R. (2002). *JIm Crow Stories*. Retrieved from PBS:

http://www.pbs.org/wnet/jimcrow/stories_events_tulsa .html

About the Author

DARRYL SMITH JR. is the author of *Life in Our Black Skin* and a veteran of the United States Army. He served ten years before leaving the military to pursue his dreams of becoming a real-estate broker. Darryl is seeking his bachelor's degree in business management at Thomas Edison State College. He wrote his first book because he felt it was necessary to voice how societal issues affect his daily living. He resides in Killeen, Texas, with his wife and kids.

About the Book

AMERICA'S LONG, DEEP-ROOTED problem will continue to grow if we continue to keep feeding it.

While the days of slavery are over, racism still remains in more prevalent forms—from police brutality to workplace discrimination to stereotyping to institutional prejudice.

It's time for Americans to stop being blind to their own ways and to become better citizens toward one another in order to defeat racism.

Author Darryl Smith Jr. challenges readers to step out of their clouded judgment so they can notice certain behaviors in the black community that needs to change, have stronger relationships within communities, and to improve the training of our police force.

We need to start a dialogue about racism so we can finally heal as a nation.

Through extended research, modern-day examples of oppression, and real-life stories from victims of racism, *Life in Our Black Skin* paints an unbiased perspective on racial tension in America.